In the Pit
and
Pop, Pop, Pop!

Level 1 – Pink

Helpful Hints for Reading at Home

The graphemes (written letters) and phonemes (units of sound) used throughout this series are aligned with Letters and Sounds. This offers a consistent approach to learning whether reading at home or in the classroom.

HERE IS A LIST OF PHONEMES FOR THIS PHASE OF LEARNING. AN EXAMPLE OF THE PRONUNCIATION CAN BE FOUND IN BRACKETS.

Phase 2			
s (sat)	a (cat)	t (tap)	p (tap)
i (pin)	n (net)	m (man)	d (dog)
g (go)	o (sock)	c (cat)	k (kin)
ck (sack)	e (elf)	u (up)	r (rabbit)
h (hut)	b (ball)	f (fish)	ff (off)
l (lip)	ll (ball)	ss (hiss)	

HERE ARE SOME WORDS WHICH YOUR CHILD MAY FIND TRICKY.

Phase 2 Tricky Words			
the	to	I	no
go	into		

GPC focus: /m/d/g/o/

TOP TIPS FOR HELPING YOUR CHILD TO READ:

- Allow children time to break down unfamiliar words into units of sound and then encourage children to string these sounds together to create the word.

- Encourage your child to point out any focus phonics when they are used.

- Read through the book more than once to grow confidence.

- Ask simple questions about the text to assess understanding.

- Encourage children to use illustrations as prompts.

This book focuses on the phonemes /m/, /d/, /g/ and /o/ and is a pink level 1 book band.

In the Pit
and
Pop, Pop, Pop!

Written by
Georgie Tennant

Illustrated by
Irene Renon

Can you say this sound and draw it with your finger?

In the Pit

Written by
Georgie Tennant

Illustrated by
Irene Renon

The tin in the pit.

Sam sat. Sam is sad.

Sam got a pot.

The pot on the tin.

Sam sat. Sam is mad.

Sam got a pan.

The dog in the pit.

Sam and the pan.

Dad in the pit!

Can you say this sound and draw it with your finger?

Pop, Pop, Pop!

Written by
Georgie Tennant

Illustrated by
Irene Renon

Tim got a pan.

Dad got a pot.

"Sit in the gap, Tim."

Tim sat. Dad got a pip.

Tip it in the pan.

Pop! Pop! Pop!

It is at the top.

It got on the gas.

"Dip it in, Tim."

"Do not gag, Dad."

Tog is on the mat.

It is in Tog!

©2021 **BookLife Publishing Ltd.**
King's Lynn, Norfolk PE30 4LS

ISBN 978-1-83927-420-6

All rights reserved. Printed in Malaysia.
A catalogue record for this book is available from the British Library.

In the Pit & Pop, Pop, Pop!
Written by Georgie Tennant
Illustrated by Irene Renon

An Introduction to BookLife Readers...

Our Readers have been specifically created in line with the London Institute of Education's approach to book banding and are phonetically decodable and ordered to support each phase of Letters and Sounds.

Each book has been created to provide the best possible reading and learning experience. Our aim is to share our love of books with children, providing both emerging readers and prolific page-turners with beautiful books that are guaranteed to provoke interest and learning, regardless of ability.

BOOK BAND GRADED using the Institute of Education's approach to levelling.

PHONETICALLY DECODABLE supporting each phase of Letters and Sounds.

EXERCISES AND QUESTIONS to offer reinforcement and to ascertain comprehension.

BEAUTIFULLY ILLUSTRATED to inspire and provoke engagement, providing a variety of styles for the reader to enjoy whilst reading through the series.

AUTHOR INSIGHT:
GEORGIE TENNANT

Georgie Tennant is a freelance writer who has written multiple stories for BookLife Publishing. She always knew she would be a writer as she used to present her school teachers with lengthy stories and poems for them to enjoy! Her two sons provide plenty of entertaining material for her writing, which usually appears on her blog or in the local newspaper as the 'Thought for the Week'. When she isn't writing she is working as a part-time secondary school English teacher, where she has the joy of inspiring slightly bigger children with the joy of reading good stories. She hopes to write good stories for them one day too.

This book focuses on the phonemes /m/, /d/, /g/ and /o/ and is a pink level 1 book band.